I Loved Her First

Published in Nashville, Tennessee, by Thomas Nelson, Inc.

Project Editor: Lisa Stilwell

Designed by Koechel Peterson Design, Minneapolis, Minnesota

ISBN-10: 1-4041-0454-2
ISBN-13: 978-1-4041-0454-9

Printed and bound in the United States

www.thomasnelson.com

I Loved Her First

Fathers' and Daughters' Cherished Memories

BY WALT ALDRIDGE AND ELLIOTT PARK

Published by
THOMAS NELSON™
Since 1798

www.thomasnelson.com

Presented To:

_____

From:

_____

Date:

_____

During my almost thirty years of writing songs for a living, I have been blessed to have had some recorded, and some of those even became popular. But I have learned that it is an altogether different experience when one of those songs actually touches people in a deeply personal way. Those songs become a part of who a writer is perceived as being, and they set the standard of what people now expect from that writer.

Having offered that insight into songwriting, I have to say that I always believed in "I Loved Her First," but that is not uncommon for me or any other songwriter. In fact, most of us think that the songs we compose are great and that the world is a somehow smaller place for not yet realizing it. We are, of course, usually dead wrong about our music, and—stuck as we are in the tiny boxes of ego where we live—our vision is simply myopic.

But very early in the release of Heartland's debut album *I Loved Her First*, it became obvious that the title song was pecking its way out of its eggshell and was about to flap its wings and take off. People began to call and e-mail to tell me how special that song was. Having experienced records that flopped as opposed to those that flapped, I felt the kind of exhilaration you feel when your child finally pedals off on a bike without the training wheels. I knew that I couldn't stop what was about to happen even if I wanted to.

Watching the song take flight was even more exciting because a new group was able to stand up and be counted along with my song. For me, that fact is probably as good as any part of the entire experience: I liked knowing that we were all leaving the runway together.

The "I Loved Her First" phenomenon has been wonderfully exhilarating and rewarding, but tomorrow morning I will do what I always do: wake up, have two cups of coffee, shower, go to my office, sit down with the third (and maybe most important) cup of coffee, and start trying to say something with words and music. If I am very blessed, at some point in my career a song will again connect with hearts. If not, I have at least had a part in one that makes me proud. Especially when I hear stories like the ones in this book.

Whether you are a dad or a daughter, a mom or a son, I hope these stories make you stop to think. Sometimes the wheels of life seem hard to face and even harder to deal with. In those times I find that something as small as the right song can help grease the axle.

Walt Aldridge

Look at the two of you

dancing that way

Lost in the moment

and each other's face

So much in love you're

alone in this place

Like there's
nobody else in the world

Proud Beyond Belief

The first time I heard "I Loved Her First," I was talking on the phone with my nineteen-year-old daughter, Kellie. She was driving in her car, taking a different route back to college four hours away, and was asking me for directions when the song came on her radio. While we were talking on our cell phones, she asked me to listen to this new song that she really liked. My eyes started tearing up. From that moment on, "I Loved Her First" was our song. Every time the song comes on her radio, she calls me and says, "Hey, Dad, our song is on," and we listen to it together.

I know that every father thinks his daughter is the most precious thing in the world, but Kellie is even more of a blessing to me because she is a cancer survivor. Kellie was only two years old when she was diagnosed with leukemia. She underwent three and a half years of chemotherapy and fifteen radiation treatments. I grew to greatly respect Kellie's strength during this struggle. She knew she was fighting a life-threatening illness, and she fought it valiantly. One Christmas, despite the fact that she was bald and sick, she said, "Look at me, Daddy! I'm riding my bicycle!" I thought, *It's amazing how much joy and pride one little child can bring.* Now she is a beautiful, intelligent college sopho-more studying to be a nurse, so she can help other sick children like those nurses who helped her when she was sick. She continues to bring me great joy and pride.

And that joy started at the very beginning of her life. I was the first one to hold Kellie when she was born. Later I held her as she underwent her treatments and suf-fered the side effects. And I held her up as she learned to ride a bicycle. I have held

her up in prayer every night since she was born. I think of her every single day and talk to her on the phone almost as often. I brag about her every opportunity I get. I am proud of her beyond belief. Nothing brightens my day quicker than to hear her say, "Hi, Daddy!" If you ask me, whoever marries her will be the luckiest man on earth.

And, yes, letting go of my little girl and putting her hand into the hand of her new husband will be one of the most difficult things I'll ever have to do. "I Loved Her First" puts into words the feelings I've had whenever I've thought about Kellie getting married. It certainly will be hard to give her away, and I pray that God will protect her and bless her in marriage just as He has protected her and blessed her to this point in her life.

A brief postscript… To make the song even more special to me, I recently found out it was written by Elliott Park, who was a track athlete at McMurry University, where I was his coach. My wife would bring Kellie to the track to visit me while Elliott worked out. He knew her when she was going through the rough times. He and I spent many hours on the road together going to track meets, and I'm sure he heard more than a few Kellie stories. Now he has written a song, inspired by his own daughter, that means the world to me and mine. Thank you, Elliott.

Craig (Coach) Agnew

I was enough for her

not long ago

I was her number one,

she told me so

Together In Spirit

It's amazing how many people have come up to me after perform-
ances or have sought me out to tell me that this song has been
meaningful to them. I remember, for instance, a letter I received
from a young woman, an only child who had lost her father a couple of years earlier. One day as she drove home from an especially
difficult day at work, she heard the song on the radio. She told me
that it was as if her father were right there with her singing each
word to her. It gave her great comfort to know that he would be
with her in spirit when that special wedding day came for her.

What more could a music creator ever aspire to than that?
Knowing that I have been a part of a positive, life-changing experience for someone makes all those hours of searching for song
ideas more than worthwhile.

Walt Aldridge

And she still means the world to me

just so you know

So be careful

when you hold my girl

The Song Says It Perfectly

Our daughter Jenna was a real "miracle" baby. Four years before Jenna was born, doctors had told my wife Lisa that she could no longer have children. Well, Jenna quickly became Daddy's girl, and for the first time in my life I felt the special love only a daughter can give her daddy. Through her middle school and high school years, Jenna built houses with me, played softball with me, and even attempted some very challenging mountain-bike trails just to spend time with Dad. She was everything I could ever ask for in a daughter. Jenna was a true blessing from God.

My wife, Lisa, and I were very proud of her when she graduated from college in the top 3 percent of her class, and we threw a big graduation party before she headed off to medical school in California. That was both the best day and the worst day of my life, because Jenna's boyfriend Chris asked me for her hand in marriage just before the party began. I didn't know what to say, but I knew Chris was a wonderful guy and the answer to all of my daughter's dreams. I was excited about saying yes to Chris, but I couldn't help but feel something inside me being ripped away.

The wedding plans began, and I found myself unable to get excited. I couldn't put my finger on it, but I felt like Chris had taken my best friend away from me. I struggled with the thought of losing my daughter. Life became a roller coaster for me. I was full of joy at one moment, but that moment would end in tears. At one point I thought I would not be able to give Jenna away at the wedding without breaking down in tears. *Why can't I be happy about this special day? This is my daughter's dream come true. Why, why, why?* I didn't have the answer.

Now, I'm not a huge country-music fan, but for some reason I had a local country station on that day when "I Loved Her First" came on. The music caught my ear. As I listened to the lyrics, I immediately broke down in tears and cried. I couldn't believe that someone had written a song that expressed my feelings exactly… Those feelings I'd been struggling to understand and hadn't been able to express had just come out over the radio!

I *was* happy that Jenna had found her life partner in Chris, but I wanted Chris to know that I loved her first and that giving her to him will not be easy. That night I e-mailed the lyrics to Jenna and asked her to read the words to Chris. That very evening, we decided "I Loved Her First" by Heartland would be our father-daughter dance song!

Now I can share the joy of planning Jenna's marriage. I owe it all to the song that helped me understand my feelings. I've never had a song touch my heart so deeply. No, giving Jenna away won't be easy, but it will be much easier now that everyone, including me, knows how I feel. Most importantly, now Chris knows "I Loved Her First"!

Philip Hughes

I loved her first

I held her first

A place in my heart
will always be hers

From the first breath
she breathed

When she first smiled at me

I knew the love of a father
runs deep

The Man Who Loved Me First

Three weeks before my wedding, my father had an aortic aneurysm rupture. When the rupture occurred, he was fortunate to be in the hospital emergency room. Although he was in a doctor's care while it happened, he had only a 20 percent chance of surviving the emergency surgery they rushed him into. It was a heart-wrenching five hours before we heard the news that they were preparing a room for him in intensive care. He had made it! He spent two weeks in ICU and another week in a regular hospital room before being released from the hospital the afternoon before the wedding.

Our wedding ceremony took place at my parents' home. My father had built the house, and I could think of no better place to start our married life. I consider the beautiful home I grew up in to be the most tangible evidence of my father's labor of love for his family. It was heartbreaking to imagine him not being there with us. Thank God, that wasn't the case.

On the day of our wedding, my father was still extremely weak. But he had enough energy to both walk me down the aisle and have our father-daughter dance. We danced to "I Loved Her First" by Heartland. That song will forever remind me of one of the happiest moments of my life. The words in that song are so meaningful by themselves, but after coming close to losing the man who did love me first, they meant even more.

Samantha Uphold

I prayed that she'd find you someday

But it's still hard
to give her away 'cause

I loved her first

I Played It First

Little did I know the song I played at my daughter's wedding would soon become a number one song...

The words brought tears to my eyes as I danced with Ashley. The message so vividly expressed what I was feeling. I knew life would never be the same. Memories of our life together and our love for each other filled my mind. Yet I had to let her go.

The song "I Loved Her First" was tenderly heart-wrenching at that moment. I had prayed over, loved, cared for, and protected Ashley first, but now my new son-in-law, Cody, was her number one man. My little girl had grown up. Knowing their love for each other, though, gave me peace.

Endgate Hawk

How could that beautiful woman

with you

be the same little freckle faced kid

that I knew?

The one that I read all those

fairytales to

And tucked into bed

all those nights

A Mom's Point of View

I know the song is written from a dad's perspective on his daughter, but we moms also have a hard time watching our kids grow up, fall in love, and get married. I want nothing more than for each of my daughters to be loved and cherished by a wonderful man, but it's still hard to watch them go.

When I hear "I Loved Her First," I also wonder how I'll feel when my son, Daniel, is grown up and gets married. Like little boys will do, he used to tell me he'd marry me when he gets big. So it's hard to imagine him finding a lovely girl, getting married, and leaving. At this point, I can't even imagine his first dance or first kiss!

This beautiful song reaches many hearts, and it will for a long time to come. I know it will never stop bringing a tear to my eye.

Laurie Moulaison

I knew the first time I saw you
with her

It was only a matter of time, but...

I loved her first
I held her first

A place in my heart will always be hers

From the first breath
she breathed

When she first smiled at me

I knew the love of a father
runs deep

A Song for New Beginnings

When I was very young, my uncle Billy and his wife moved to Atlanta and took their daughter, my cousin, Rachel with them. They divorced a couple of years afterward.

Billy has always been a very quiet man who stayed to himself. He helped raise his daughter—she has never had to go without anything—but Billy had a very hard time after the divorce, and he drank a lot while Rachel was growing up.

About three years ago, Rachel started dating a young man who convinced her to go to church, and shortly afterward she convinced her dad to quit drinking. Billy even started going to a small church close to where he lives.

About six months ago Rachel told me that she and Jake are getting married. She wants to have a father/daughter dance, but her dad doesn't dance, plus she couldn't find the right song. Not long after that I called Rachel and Billy and played "I Loved Her First" over the phone. They both cried and wanted to know if I could get the song. Not only did I get it, I waited in the meet-and-greet line at the Big Spring Jam and got the boys to autograph the actual CD that will be played at the wedding reception!

One more thing… Uncle Billy is secretly taking dance lessons so he can dance with Rachel to this song. We can't wait, because we know this will be a very special day for them both.

Donna Duncan

Someday you might know what
I'm going through

When a miracle smiles up at you

I loved her first

I prayed that she'd find
you someday

But it's still hard to give her away 'cause

I loved her first
I held her first

A place in my heart will always be hers

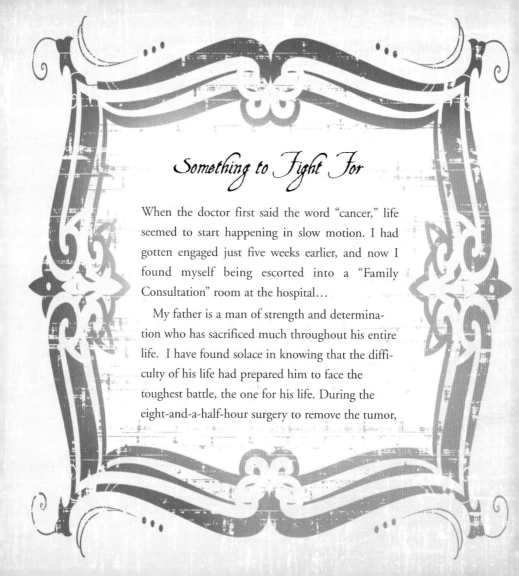

Something to Fight For

When the doctor first said the word "cancer," life seemed to start happening in slow motion. I had gotten engaged just five weeks earlier, and now I found myself being escorted into a "Family Consultation" room at the hospital…

My father is a man of strength and determination who has sacrificed much throughout his entire life. I have found solace in knowing that the difficulty of his life had prepared him to face the toughest battle, the one for his life. During the eight-and-a-half-hour surgery to remove the tumor,

I think that my mom wore a hole in the carpet with her pacing. Dad made it through the surgery with flying colors—but we were naive to think that the hard part was behind him.

Dad's road to recovery was anything but easy. But through all this, my family and I truly learned that God will not give us anything we can't endure and that we can bear the burden more easily when we do it together…

The first time I ever heard "I Loved Her First," I called my dad right afterward to tell him I'd heard the song we would dance to at my wedding, and I could tell he was smiling. I bought Heartland's CD the day he was diagnosed with cancer and have listened to the song every day since. When I feel like the world is spiraling out of control, the song gives me peace.

During this incredibly strenuous time, I commented on Heartland's Myspace.com page. The next day I received a comment back from them telling me that my father and my family would be in their prayers. I continuously prayed for my dad, specifically that I would be able to dance with him at the free concert Heartland was doing near my hometown a few weeks from then—and my prayers were answered. Not only did my dad and I get to meet the band after the show, but they signed my CD and listened to my story of what their music has meant to me. [Drummer] Todd [Anderson] even told me that he had to look away during "I Loved Her First" because my dad and I were making him teary eyed.

Every day is an uphill battle, and my father still has chemotherapy and radiation ahead of him. Even though my father's cancer—more aggressive than originally thought—has spread to his lymph nodes, we are all able to keep our heads up high. For me, that is possible largely because of this amazing song. The song also reminds my father that he has something to fight for because his daughter still needs him.

Every girl dreams of her dad walking her down the aisle. My wedding day will just not work without my dad to give me away. I have faith that my prayers for my dad will be answered and that God will allow my wedding-day dream to come true—my dream of going around the dance floor with Dad to "I Loved Her First."

Nicole Salie

From the first breath
she breathed

When she first smiled at me

I knew the love of a father
runs deep

I prayed that she'd find you
someday

But it's still hard
to give her away

I loved her first

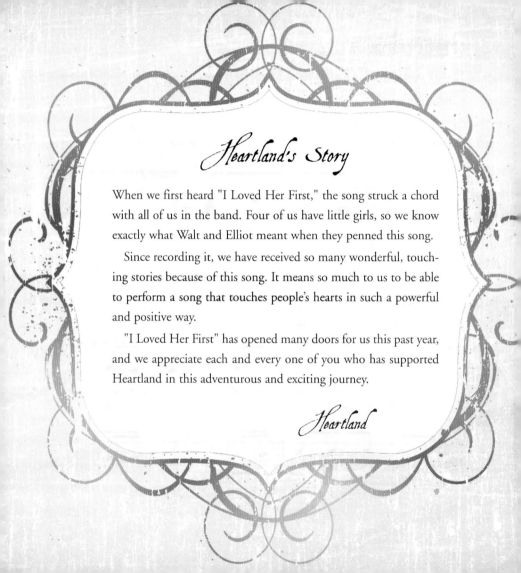

Heartland's Story

When we first heard "I Loved Her First," the song struck a chord with all of us in the band. Four of us have little girls, so we know exactly what Walt and Elliot meant when they penned this song.

Since recording it, we have received so many wonderful, touching stories because of this song. It means so much to us to be able to perform a song that touches people's hearts in such a powerful and positive way.

"I Loved Her First" has opened many doors for us this past year, and we appreciate each and every one of you who has supported Heartland in this adventurous and exciting journey.

Heartland

The Little Song That Could

People often ask me what inspired "I Loved Her First." I usually tell them what I know they want to hear—that the idea came to me shortly after my daughter's birth and that all those new fatherly feelings I was experiencing resulted in the song. And that's true, but there's more to the story…

In 2002, after the birth of my first daughter, Anna, I had a concept for a song. I wrote these two lines: "I loved her first. I held her first." Along with these words, two measures of a simple waltz melody popped into my head. And that's it. For a year and a half, that idea lay dormant in a massive pile of other song ideas in the very back of my mind.

In late January 2004, I made a trip to Nashville for a week of cowriting and recording. Two months earlier I had signed with Extreme Writers Group, an independent publisher in Nashville. Jason Houser and Michael Martin, co-owners of Extreme, had scheduled the cowrites, and I was very excited but very nervous because I had never written a song with anybody. My first cowrite was Tuesday morning with veteran songwriter Walt Aldridge. I remember sitting at the piano in the writing room

waiting for Walt to show up, and when he did—at about 10:20—I was a mess of nerves.

Walt sat down and we chatted awhile as he picked at his guitar. After a few minutes I managed to calm down a little. Then he asked me, "You got any ideas today?"

It's sort of the unwritten rule in Nashville that the less-experienced writer brings the concepts to the table, so I quickly pulled out what I thought were my best ideas. We knocked them around awhile, but nothing really sparked. Sometimes a cowrite just never gets off the ground, and the first warning sign is usually the presence of more dead air than creative air. We were dangerously close to that awkward point when I reached into my satchel and found the piece of paper I had written those two lines on so many months before.

"Well, Walt," I said, "here's an idea I've had for a couple of years, but I don't know where to go with it." I played him the first few measures of the chorus idea I had—and he jumped on it. I remember him saying, "That's our idea. Let's go with that one." Basically, the song was finished later that afternoon.

We both knew right away it was a hit. We played it for Michael and Jason, and they knew it was a hit, but it took two years of pitching before the song found a home with Heartland and Lofton Creek. I don't know exactly why it was passed up so many times. Maybe there was a fear of portraying the artist as being old enough to have a grown daughter. Or maybe it was just the standard fear of slow waltzes.

Finally, in May 2006, I got this e-mail from Jason Houser:

> *Elliott,*
>
> *Hello, my friend.*
>
> *You have some press on Music Row. Looks like you've got an independent label single coming out on "I Loved Her First."*
>
> *The label head said it is one of the most moving songs that he has ever heard.... Pretty good stuff.*
>
> *I hope you're doing well.*
>
> *Write on,*
>
> *Jason*

I must be perfectly honest. I had no idea who Heartland was. I had never heard them or even heard of them. All I knew was that they weren't Tim McGraw, or George Strait, or anybody else I thought should sing the song. I was a little down, but that didn't last long.

Within a few weeks, the stir began. Within a few more weeks, the stir grew to a buzz. And we all know what happened. What many do not know, though, is that "I Loved Her First" was my first number one hit, my first top 40 hit, my first single release, and, technically, my first song to ever get cut. It was also my first cowrite. (We haven't

checked the record books, but this song may have set one!) "I Loved Her First" was also Heartland's first cut on the album and first single release. Needless to say, several people ventured into a lot of uncharted territory with this song. And that's one of the things that made this whole experience so great. Everything about this song has been wonderful for me. Watching Heartland race up the charts, zigzagging up through the established giants like some Seabiscuit of the music world, and eventually hitting that number one spot was something I'll never forget. And considering all that this song has meant to so many people... Well, the experience has been just incredible.

I thank God for the plan He had for this song and for the hearts He has touched with it. I thank God that Walt didn't settle for those mediocre ideas I pulled out first and that he recognized those two scribbled lines for what they eventually grew into. I have a feeling that nothing I ever write again will be quite like "I Loved Her First." Or—as I have heard it referred to—the little song that could.

Elliott Park

CEDAR MUSIC PUBLISHING LLC

Extreme Writers Group and *Cedar Music Publishing* are partners in a music publishing and content development company based in Nashville, Tennessee.

Our mission is to positively influence lives through the power of music and inspire creators to perform at their highest level.

For more information about our companies and products, go to:

www.extremewritersgroup.com

Bringing families together and encouraging
them to live lives of worship and prayer.

www.seedsfamilyworship.com